To _____

From _____

Other books by Exley:
Daughters …
Sisters …
True Love …

Published simultaneously in 1995 by Exley Publications in Great Britain, and
Exley Giftbooks in the USA.
Copyright © Helen Exley 1995

12 11 10 9 8 7 6 5 4 3 2 1

Border illustrations by Juliette Clarke
Edited and pictures selected by Helen Exley

ISBN 1-85015-690-5

Designed by Pinpoint Design.
Picture research by P. A. Goldberg and J. M. Clift, Image Select, London.
Typeset by Delta, Watford.
Printed and bound by Tien Wah Ltd., Singapore

Exley Publications Ltd, 16 Chalk Hill, Watford, Herts. WD1 4BN.
Exley Giftbooks, 232 Madison Avenue, Suite 1206, NY 10016, USA.

$\mathscr{M}$ISSING YOU...

QUOTATIONS SELECTED BY
$\mathscr{H}$ELEN EXLEY

≣EXLEY
NEW YORK · WATFORD UK

You cannot believe how much I miss you. I love you so much, and we are not used to separation. So I stay awake most of the night thinking of you, and by day I find my feet carrying me ... to your room ... then finding it empty I depart, as sick and sorrowful as a lover locked out.

PLINY THE YOUNGER,
(1ST CENTURY A.D.),
TO HIS WIFE CALPURNIA

Nice girl, good girl, lovely girl, adorable girl – oh adjective adjective adjective Frances, what in the hell did you have to go away for? I know that before putting up a big building they always rip a huge hole in the ground for the foundations – but I don't need to have one ripped in me to make the structure of my love secure – it's rooted deep in me already; it won't even die with me, but will outlive me by always and, if you aren't too sleepy, five minutes.

OGDEN NASH (1902-1971),
IN A LETTER TO FRANCES LEONARD IN 1930

I must see her [Josephine] and press her to my heart. I love her to the point of madness, and I cannot continue to be separated from her. If she no longer loved me, I would have nothing left to do on earth.

NAPOLEON BONAPARTE (1769-1821),
IN A LETTER TO HIS BROTHER

Love is you and love is me
Love is a prison and love is free
Love's what's there when you're
away from me.

ADRIAN HENRI, b.1932,
FROM "LOVE IS..."

I see the world more vividly
because I am harvesting the days
for you. Oddities, marvels –
something beautiful, something
strange. I collect them for you.
And, sharing them, discover them
anew.

PAM BROWN, b.1928

Darling, my darling, One line in haste to tell you that I love you more today than ever in my life before, that I never see beauty without thinking of you or scent happiness without thinking of you. You have fulfilled all my ambition, realized all my hopes, made all my dreams come true.

SIR ALFRED DUFF COOPER (1890-1954),
TO HIS FUTURE WIFE DIANA

I long for you, as one
Whose dhow in summer winds
is blown adrift and lost,
Longs for the land, and finds –
Again the compass tells –
A grey and empty sea.

SOMALI POEM

Two that have loved, and now divided far,
Bound by loves bond, in heart together are.

WALOFRED STRABO (809-849)

When you have gone away,
No flowers more, methinks, will be –
No maple leaves in all the world –
Till you come back to me.

YANAGIWARA YASU-KO (1783-1866)

Places that are empty of you ...
are empty of all life.

DANTE GABRIEL ROSSETTI (1828-1882)

You do not speak
you do not come

the hall flows shadows

    I am a room
    sealed in stone

the fire is ash
warmth will not return

    I am frost   I am ice
    I splinter   I burn

GRACE PERRY,
FROM "SNOW IN SUMMER"

I have a thousand images of you in an hour; all
different and all coming back to the same…. And
we love. And we've got the most amazing secrets
and understandings. Noël, whom I love, who is
so beautiful and wonderful. I think of you eating
omelette on the ground. I think of you once
against a sky line: and on the hill that Sunday
morning. And that night was wonderfullest of all.
The light and shadow & quietness & the rain &
the wood. And you…. Your arms and lips and
hair and shoulders and voice – you.

RUPERT BROOKE (1887-1915), *TO NOËL OLIVIER.
BROOKE WAS KILLED DURING WORLD WAR I*

I am lying here worn out, among
the remotest tribes and regions....
And ... you, my wife ... occupy
more than your equal share in my
heart. My voice names you only; no
night, no day comes to me without
you ... your name is ever on my
wandering lips.... Tears sometimes
have the weight of words.

OVID (43 B.C. – 18 A.D.)

My Heart – We are thus far
separated – but after all one mile is
as bad as a thousand – which is a
great consolation to one who must
travel six hundred before he meets
you again. – If it will give you any
satisfaction – I am as comfortless as
a pilgrim with peas in his shoes –
and as cold as Charity – Chastity
or any other Virtue.

LORD BYRON (1788-1824)

Out of the depths of my happy heart wells a great tide of love & prayer for this priceless treasure that is confided to my life-long keeping. You cannot see its intangible waves as they flow toward you, darling, but in these lines you will hear, as it were, the distant beating of its surf.

Paris is a morgue without you: before I knew you, it was Paris, and I thought it was heaven; but now it is a vast desert of desolation and loneliness. It is like the face of a clock, bereft of its hands.

SARAH BERNHARDT (1844-1923),
IN A LETTER TO VICTORIEN SARDOU

Do you read these jogged scrawls, I
wonder. I think of your poor eyes, and
resolve to tear what I have written up:
then I look out at the ghostly country
and the beautiful night, and I cannot
bring myself to read a miserable
book.... Yes, as you guess, Ellen, I am
having a bad attack of you just at
present. I am restless; and a man's
restlessness always means a woman;
and my restlessness means Ellen.

GEORGE BERNARD SHAW (1856-1930),
TO ELLEN TERRY

COUNTRY POEM

Owls were hooting when I went to bed
And when I got up blackbirds were singing
and I hadn't slept at all in between
Thinking about you.

ADRIAN HENRI, b.1932

The moon hath sunk, and the Pleiades
And midnight is gone,
And the hour is passing, passing,
And I lie alone.

SAPPHO

I shall fold my arms together,
after I am in bed,
and try to imagine
that you are close to my heart.
Naughty wife,
what right have you
to be anywhere else?
How many sweet words
I should breathe into your ear,
in the quiet night —
how many holy kisses
would I press
upon your lips....

NATHANIEL HAWTHORNE (1804–1864),
TO HIS FIANCEE SOPHIA PEABODY

There is something beautiful even on the
battlefields of France, and these roses I have
plucked for you, which were struggling
to live among the nettles and thorns of
this desolated village.
As they have lived, so you must live and
lift up your heart when the world is lonely and sad,
and after all, there is something beautiful in this
troubled universe of ours.

CAPTAIN FRED HARDMAN,
TO HIS WIFE KIT, DURING WORLD WAR I

I'm altogether immersed in the happiness I derive from seeing you. Nothing else counts.… Not only am I not sad, I'm even deeply happy and secure. Even the tenderest memories – of all your dear expressions, or your little arms cradling the pillow in the morning – aren't painful to me. I feel myself all enfolded and sustained by your love.

SIMONE DE BEAUVOIR (1908-1986),
TO JEAN-PAUL SARTRE

Write to me only once a week so that your letter arrives on Sunday – for I cannot endure your daily letters. I am incapable of enduring them. For instance, I answer one of your letters, then lie in bed in apparent calm, but my heart beats through my entire body and is conscious only of you. I belong to you; there is really no other way of expressing it, and that is not strong enough. But for this very reason I don't want to know what you are wearing; it confuses me so much that I cannot deal with life …

FRANZ KAFKA (1883-1924), *TO FELICE BAUER*

*Have you forgotten me? I am the man
you used to say you loved. I used to
sleep in your arms – do you remember?
But you never write. You are perhaps
mindless of me. I am not of you. I love
you. There isn't a moment of any
hideous day when I do not say to myself,
"It will be alright. I shall go home.
Caitlin loves me. I love Caitlin." But
perhaps you have forgotten. If you have
forgotten, or lost your affection for me,
please, my Cat, let me know. I Love You.
Dylan.*

DYLAN THOMAS (1914-1953)

What then do you do all day, Madame? What business is so vital that it robs you of the time to write to your faithful lover? What attachment can be stifling and pushing aside the love, the tender and constant love which you promised him? ... Beware, Josephine; one fine night the doors will be broken down and there I shall be.

NAPOLEON BONAPARTE (1769-1821),
TO HIS WIFE JOSEPHINE DE BEAUHARNAIS

*A*ll the time I have been thinking of an armchair made for two, in front of a huge crackling fire, the wireless playing some tuneful tunes, and the firelight making shadows on the walls.

Fire watching night!

a hectic ruff and tumble and then sweet reconciliation.

a terribly beautiful hug and then clasped in your arms, my head on your breast,

something I am longing for now, a kiss that makes time stand still.

PAMELA MOORE,
TO HER FUTURE HUSBAND CORRADO RUFFONI

I don't think I can properly wait [for your return] until my picture is done. My hands tremble so I can scarcely write, and my head is swimming. It would be much better if I didn't tell you all this but I am past all control. Tell me when I might come, and I would come with the small picture and paint there. It would not be fair to keep us [apart] till July past [sic]. You musn't be upset. I only tell you what should be a sense of congratulation to yourself that you are so much in my thoughts. I can draw occasionally, but I know I couldn't paint a bit…. As the chance approaches of seeing and living with you I grow more impatient.

JOHN EVERETT MILLAIS (1829-1896),
TO HIS WIFE EUPHEMIA

I have not spent a day without loving you; I have not spent a night without embracing you; I have not so much as drunk a single cup of tea without cursing the pride and ambition which force me to remain separated from the moving spirit of my life. In the midst of my duties, whether I am at the head of my army or inspecting the camps, my beloved Josephine stands alone in my heart, occupies my mind, fills my thoughts.

NAPOLEON BONAPARTE (1769-1821),
IN A LETTER TO JOSEPHINE BONAPARTE

… High heaven causes a girl's lovelonging.
It is like being too far from the light,
Far from the hearth of familiar arms …

UNKNOWN EGYPTIAN, FROM
"LOVE OF YOU IS MIXED DEEP IN MY VITALS"

Whatever I am doing, wherever I am going, whatever I am planning, you are there. I try to persuade you to wait patiently at the edges of my mind, but you invade me. You are in the very air: I meet you at every turn.

PAM BROWN, b.1928

I did not know
how huge and hollow dark can be,
how cold the light.
I walk away
towards the turning of a key,
a chair, a cat,
the automatic making of a cup of tea.
The compromise that's life
till you come back to me.

PAM BROWN, b.1928.
EXTRACT FROM "LOVE".

Even nights when I sleep alone
I set the pillows side by side:
One is my love –
Holding it close, I sleep.

JAPANESE FOLK SONG

Parting is bitter and weeping vain,
And all true lovers will meet again,
And no fate can sever my love from me,
For his heart is the river and mine the sea.

IRISH SONG

The breeze is blowing
Towards the open sea at Turanga,
You are far away, my dear
My love goes out to you from here.

My love falls like the rain
On the open sea at Turanga
I am left behind here
Living with my love for you.

MAORI SONG

THE HOUSE GROWN SILENT

After he had gone the wind rose,
Buffeting the house and rumbling in the chimney,
And I thought; It will roar against him like a lion
As onward he goes.

Seven miles before him, all told –
Chilled will be the lips I kissed so warm at parting,
Kissed in vain; for he's forth in the wind, and kisses
Won't keep out the cold.

Closer should I have kissed, and fondlier prayed:
Pleasant is the room in the wakeful firelight,
And within is the bed, arrayed with peace and safety.
Would he had stayed!

SYLVIA TOWNSEND WARNER (1893-1978)

THE DOOR

When she came suddenly in
It seemed the door could never close again,
Nor even did she close it – she, she –
The room lay open to a visiting sea
Which no door could restrain.

Yet when at last she smiled, tilting her head
To take her leave of me,
Where she had smiled, instead
There was a dark door closing endlessly,
The waves receded.

ROBERT GRAVES (1895-1985)

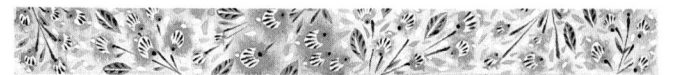

I'm afraid I shan't get used to this emptiness. Do you remember how often I used to tell you that I never really believed I had you? Every morning when I woke up it was a glorious amazement to find that I really did, and to see your head on the next pillow, and to stretch out my hand and touch you. Now it's just the opposite. When I wake, I can't believe that you aren't there; I can't look at a doorway without thinking that you must presently walk through it, I can't enter a room without hoping to find you sitting in it.... And at the same time I know it can't happen, and darling, darling, that's an appalling knowledge.

OGDEN NASH (1902-1971),
IN A LETTER TO HIS WIFE IN 1935

Absence is a short kind of death.

ALEXANDER POPE (1688-1744)

Only three things are infinite: the sky in its stars, the sea in its drops of water, and the heart in its tears.

GUSTAVE FLAUBERT (1821-1880)

I can neither Eat nor Sleep for thinking of You my dearest love, I never touch even pudding.

HORATIO NELSON (1758-1805),
TO LADY EMMA HAMILTON

When I go away from you
The world beats dead
Like a slackened drum.
I call out for you against the jutted stars
And shout into the ridges of the wind.
Streets coming fast,
One after another,
Wedge you away from me,
And the lamps of the city prick my eyes
So that I can no longer see your face,
Why should I leave you,
To wound myself upon the sharp edges of the night?

AMY LOWELL (1874-1925), *"THE TAXI"*

... I kisse your letter. I am sure the poore paper smarts for my Idolatry, which by wearing it continually neere my brest will at last bee burnt and martyrd in those flames of adoration it hath kindled in mee.

JOHN DRYDEN
(1631-1700),
*TO HIS COUSIN,
HONOR DRYDEN*

You say that you are feeling my absence very much, and your only comfort when I am not there is to hold my writings in your hand and often put them in my place by your side. I like to think that you miss me and find relief in this sort of consolation. I, too, am always reading your letters, and returning to them again and again as if they were new to me – but this only fans the fire of my longing for you. If your letters are so dear to me, you can imagine how I delight in your company; do write as often as you can, although you give me pleasure mingled with pain.

PLINY THE YOUNGER, (1ST CENTURY A.D.),
TO HIS WIFE CALPURNIA

I look down the tracks and see you coming – and out of every haze & mist your darling rumpled trousers are hurrying to me – Without you, dearest dearest I couldn't see or hear or feel or think – or live – I love you so and I'm never in all our lives going to let us be apart another night. It's like begging for mercy of a storm or killing Beauty or growing old, without you.

ZELDA FITZGERALD (1900–1948),
TO F. SCOTT FITZGERALD

I will come back alive & as deep in

love with you as a cormorant dives,

as an anemone grows, as Neptune

breathes, as the sea is deep.

DYLAN THOMAS (1914-1953),
TO HIS WIFE CAITLIN

My love, my angel, you are gone. You were able to go away and leave me for six months! No, I shall never resist the tedium of so long an absence. It has lasted only four hours and is already insupportable.

MADAME D'EPINAY
TO HER HUSBAND

*T*HAT AFTERNOON ...

I cannot get that beautiful afternoon out of
my head, above me where I lay the grass was
silhouetted against the blue of the heavens,
small clouds were rushing past as the wind
drove them on an endless journey. Then
close to me was the most lovely of all, your
soft hair against my cheek, your kisses so
cool and unearthly and my happiness was
so great.

JULIA LEE-BOOKER
TO HER FUTURE HUSBAND
LIEUT. PAT McSWINEY, 1940

Acknowledgements: The publishers are grateful for permission to reproduce copyright material. While every effort has been made to trace copyright holders, the publishers would be pleased to hear from any not here acknowledged. SIMONE DE BEAUVOIR: extract from "Letters To Sartre", translated and edited by Quintin Hoare, from the French edition by Sylvie le Bon de Beauvoir, published by Radius, the Random Century Group, 1991. English translation © 1991 Quintin Hoare. Original French text © 1990 by Editions Gallimard; DUFF COOPER: extract from "A Durable Fire: The Letters of Duff and Diana Cooper", published by HarperCollins Publishers, © 1983 Artemis Cooper; ZELDA FITZGERALD: extract from "Zelda Fitzgerald" by Nancy Milford, published by The Bodley Head. Reprinted by permission of Laurence Pollinger Ltd. on behalf of the Estate of Zelda Fitzgerald. ROBERT GRAVES: "The Door" taken from "Collected Poems", published by Cassell, © Robert Graves 1965. Reprinted by permission of Carcanet Press and Oxford University Press Inc., New York; COLONEL FRED HARDMAN: Reprinted with permission of the copyright holders of the papers of Colonel F. Hardman, M.C. T.D. J.P. and The Imperial War Museum; ADRIAN HENRI: extracts from "Collected Poems 1967-1985", Allison and Busby 1986, © Adrian Henri 1986. Reproduced by permission of the author c/o Rogers, Coleridge and White Ltd., 20 Powis Mews, London W11 1JN; JULIA LEEBOOKER: extract from "Forces Sweethearts" by Joanna Lumley, published by Bloomsbury Publishing, 1993; OGDEN NASH: extracts from "Loving Letters from Ogden Nash", published by Little, Brown and Company, © 1990 Isabel Nash Eberstadt and Linell Nash Smith; GRACE PERRY: from "Snow in Summer", published by South Head Press, Berima © 1980; GEORGE BERNARD SHAW: extract from "Ellen Terry and Bernard Shaw", published by Max Reinhardt, London, 1931; DYLAN